EXPLORING KING ARTHUR'S BRITAIN

EXPLORING
KING ARTHUR'S
BRITAIN

DENISE STOBIE

COLLINS & BROWN

First published in Great Britain in 1999
by Collins & Brown Ltd
London House
Great Eastern Wharf
Parkgate Road
London SW11 4NQ

British Library Cataloguing in Publication Data:
A CIP catalogue record for this book is available from the British Library.

ISBN 1-85585-695-6

1 3 5 7 9 8 6 4 2

Creative director: Julian Holland
Designed by Nigel White
Origination by Colour Symphony, Singapore
Printed in Hong Kong by Hong Kong Graphic & Printing Ltd.

Photographic Acknowledgements:
Sarah Boait: Front cover, half title page, p7, p8/9, p10/11, p12/13, p14/15, p20, p21, p26, p27, p28/29, p30, p31, p32/33, p34, p35, p36/37, p38, p42/43, p44/45, p46, p48/49, p50/51, p52/53, p66, p67, p68, p69, p80/81, p83, p87, p88, p89, p90/91, p92/93, p94/95.

Julian Holland: Back cover, Title page, p5/6, p18/19, p22, p23, p24/25, p39, p40/41, p54/55, p56/57, p58, p59, p60, p61, p62, p63, , p64, p65, p70, p72/73, p74/75, p76/77, p78/79, p82, p84/85, p86.

Winchester Tourist Office: p47

Library pictures: p16, p17.

Front Cover Photograph: *St Michael's Mount, the Grail Castle of legend*
Back Cover Photograph: *Glastonbury Tor*
Half-title page: *King Arthur's profile in the cliffs of Tintagel Head*
Title Page: *Tintagel Head, Arthur's birthplace, pounded by Atlantic waves*
Contents Page: *Lantyan Wood and the valley of the River Fowey, home of Tristan*

CONTENTS

ARTHURIAN SITES INCLUDED IN THIS BOOK

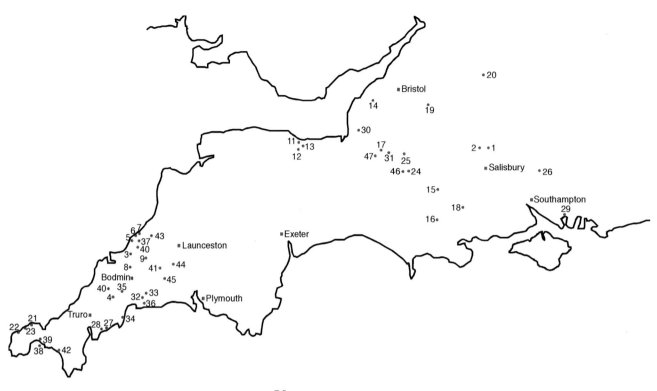

KEY TO MAP

1 Amesbury
2 Stonehenge
3 Tregeare Rounds
4 St Dennis
5 Tintagel, Merlin's Cave and
 St Julitta's Well
6 Barras Head
7 Willapark
8 Kelly Rounds
9 Arthur's Hall
10 Castle-an-Dinas
11 Dunster
12 Bat's Castle
13 Carhampton
14 Cadbury-Congresbury
15 River Divelish
16 Devil's Brook
17 St Bride's Mound, Glastonbury Tor and Abbey,
 Wearyall Hill, Wellhouse Lane and Chalice Well
18 Badbury Rings
19 Bathampton Down and Little Solsbury Hill
20 Liddington Castle
21 Zennor and Zennor Head
22 Carn Vellan
23 Trereen Dinas

24 Cadbury Castle
25 Arthur's Bridge
26 Winchester
27 Veryan Beacon
28 Dingerein
29 Portchester
30 Brent Knoll
31 Ponter's Ball
32 Castle Dore
33 Lantyan Wood and
 St Sampson-in-Golant
34 Chapel Point
35 Roche Rock
36 Tristan Stone
37 St Nechtan's Glen and Kieve
38 St Michael's Mount
39 Marazion
40 Slaughterbridge
41 Dozmary Pool
42 Loe Pool
43 Giant's Grave
44 Arthur's Bed
45 Trevethy Quoit
46 River Cam
47 'Lantokai' and Pomparles Bridge

INTRODUCTION

Artos, Artorius, Arthur. High King, Warleader, Pendragon.
Arthur, the Once and Future King.

THE NAME OF KING ARTHUR, that legendary leader of Britain, is known throughout the world, a name of mystery and legend far surpassing tales of other heroes. The fascination with Arthur, it seems, never quite fades away.

But what is the legend? In fact, there are many, many versions of the Arthurian Saga. Often, the series of tales is referred to under the catch-all title of 'The Matter of Britain', as it was referred to by the medieval minstrels and troubadors who helped make the romance of Arthur one of the most popular subjects of the day. Over the centuries, two or three versions have become `definitive', with differences only in minor details.

Here, recounted to you by a nameless storyteller, is one of them.

"Gather nearer the fire, my friends, and I shall tell to you the tale of Arthur, the king who was once – and shall be again . . .
Uther Pendragon, High King of all Britain, fell hopelessly in love with Ygraine, wife of Gorlois Duke of Cornwall. War was declared between the two men, and on a night of wind and mist and storm Uther's men besieged Gorlois at Demelioc in Cornwall. Knowing that Ygraine was housed with her servants and child at Tintagel only a short ride away, Uther travelled there under cover of magic with Merlin the Enchanter. His only aim was now to seduce Ygraine – and with sorcery, the magician transformed Uther into the likeness of Gorlois so that he was able to enter both castle and bedchamber unchallenged . . .
The next day, the dreadful news was brought to Ygraine and her daughter, Morgan, that Gorlois was dead, slaughtered at the very moment she thought she shared his bed. We cannot tell how distressed she might have been to hear how she had been

The 14th century castle at Tintagel, Cornwall, on the site of an ancient palace. Here Uther Pendragon came to Ygraine, disguised by Merlin's magic, and Arthur was conceived.

betrayed: suffice it to say, she and Uther were married in haste and the fruit of their magical union was Arthur.

On the night of his birth, as storms lashed the stronghold of Tintagel, the babe was carried away by Merlin the Magician in order to protect his Destiny. Placed into fosterage with a knight named Ector, he remained unaware of his true identity and was raised with Ector's son, Kay. At a tournament in Winchester, acting as Kay's squire, he was asked to fetch a sword which had been forgotten. Unable to find it and with time running short, he pulled a fine sword from out of a stone, or perhaps it was an anvil, and took it to his foster brother. The awed reaction stunned him, for in his haste he had failed to notice the words written on the stone: "Whomsoever pulls the sword from the stone is rightwise King of all England." We are told that Uther was dead by this time, betrayed and poisoned in Tintagel. And although many jealous knights and kings disputed his right and his title, the proof of the sword was undeniable and Arthur was duly crowned.

The sword which he had pulled from the stone served him well, until one rain-swept day it broke in his hands. Merlin, now ever by his side, took him to a great lake, and as they rowed out over the water, a hand clad in white samite rose from the waves wielding a great sword. As Arthur took this fine weapon, named Caliburn or Excalibur, he learned that it was a gift from the Lady of the Lake. There followed a great and glorious career, fighting the Saxons (or French, or Vikings, or simply other kings). He married the beautiful Guinevere, daughter of Leodegrance, and as her dowry she brought with her the legendary Round Table. He brought together the greatest knights of the kingdom at this table – knights such as Kay, Tristram, Lancelot, Bedivere, Gawain, Percival and Galahad. He watched as they undertook the Quest for the Holy Grail. He fought giants, travelled to the Underworld, undertook other quests for mystical, magical, mythical beasts, spears, combs, cups. . . .

His greatest victory came at the siege of Badon, where he defeated the Saxons and halted their westward advance for some twenty years. Britain was at peace for the first time in living memory. But there was treachery in the land and in the court itself – first Guinevere betrayed him with Lancelot, that bravest of knights; and finally, the younger knights began muttering about old men and old blood . . .

Led by Mordred, whom some claimed was Arthur's illegitimate son by his half-sister Morgan le Fay, the young knights faced the old at Camlan strand. In terrible strife, battle was joined and, as the evening mist rolled in, Arthur and Mordred finally came face to face. Tragedy! As the great king slaughtered Mordred with a mighty blow, Arthur himself was mortally wounded . . .
An era of hope was ending.

The magical sword Excalibur was returned to the Lady of the Lake by the grieving Bedivere. Arthur, bleeding from a grievous wound, was carried away on a barge to the Isle of Avalon, accompanied by three grieving queens.

But in Avalon he was healed of his wounds and, even today, he lies sleeping in a cave with his faithful knights (no-one knows where) until Britain should have need of him once more and then Arthur, once and forever, will come again."

That, then, is the legend of the great King Arthur, Christianized and Anglicized and romanticized over a thousand years or more into the version we know today.

Was there a historical Arthur? Other heroes, like Robin Hood or Wayland the Smith, may have some nebulous reality but are more likely to have been figures of pagan religions. But our Artos, Artorius, Arthur . . . . can we find some historical ground? Many books have been written on the subject

The Somerset Levels, once a lake, with Glastonbury Tor dominating the horizon.

of the 'real' Arthur, some more scholarly than others. Those readers who are interested in the subject will no doubt find at least one which makes more sense to them than others – I personally recommend the books of Geoffrey Ashe. The sources for the subject remain unchanged: the core of the major medieval legend is found in Geoffrey of Monmouth's '*History of the Kings of Britain*', itself based on a miscellany of earlier Celtic, Breton and Welsh sources; '*History of the Britons*' by Nennius, who talks mainly of Arthur's military successes; the '*Annales Cambriae*' or Welsh Annals; and the '*Complaining Book*' of Gildas, a Welsh monk living in the sixth century. These sources place the legends half a century earlier than the chivalrous romances of later days, such as Malory's '*Morte d'Arthur*' and Tennyson's 'Idylls of the King'. In fact, virtually all the scholars who believe in a 'real' Arthur place him firmly in that period of British history known as the Dark Ages, after the Romans had left British shores and before Britain became Anglo-Saxon England.

We can say that he was a warrior with a particular flair for leadership and strategy, with some knowledge of Roman warfare and probably – though without historical foundation – a great believer in the superiority of cavalry over infantry. The Roman word closest in meaning to 'knights' is *equites*, meaning horsemen: the French for knights, chevaliers, means exactly the same. At no point in the earliest versions of his story is Arthur ever called king, or even chieftain. Nennius even says that '*there were many more noble than he . . . Arthur fought against the Saxons alongside the kings of the Britons, but he himself was the leader in the battles*'. Probably, the best title we can give him is 'Dux Bellorum' – War Duke.

What then of his wife, his magician, his knights? What, indeed, of his parents?

Guinevere is a late version of the British name Gwenhwyfar. One presumes that Arthur married, and there is no reason to assume that his wife was other than young Gwen. There is, however, little or no historical basis for her existence.

Merlin was as real, historically speaking, as Arthur himself, and with as much evidence. His authenticity is beautifully explored in Nikolai Tolstoy's book '*The Quest for Merlin*'. The only problem is that some eighty years separate our best dating evidence for the two, making Arthur very old and Merlin very young if they ever met. Incidentally, according to Geoffrey Ashe, the name 'Merlin' was politely anglicised by Geoffrey of Monmouth to avoid offence. The truer spelling, Myrddin, was far too close to the French 'merde' to be repeated in polite company!

Kay and Bedivere are, in all stories, named as Arthur's closest companions. Their British names were Cei and Bedwyr, and these are the spellings I have used in the text. Other knights such as Tristram and Gawain also have a place in earlier stories, as Drustanus or Tristan and as Gwalchmai. Mordred (or, in Cornish, Modred) is named in the Welsh Annals as Medraut. King Mark of Cornwall, cuckolded husband of Yseult (Essyllt), is more shadowy. Uther Pendragon and his brother Ambrosius Aurelianus are more nebulous still: although named as the sons of Constantine III, who was a real, historical figure proclaimed Emperor by the British in 407, it seems that an ingenious medieval chronicler then blended fact and fiction until the edges blurred. Ambrosius was possibly a real soldier born of an old Romanised family, who began the campaigns against invading Saxons, Picts and Irish and who was succeeded by another, whom we call Arthur. For Gorlois and Ygraine, unfortunately, we have no real evidence at all.

The tower of St Michael's Chapel on the summit of Glastonbury Tor, veiled by Avalon mists.

Those locations named in the stories can sometimes be traced through modern place-name evidence, although occasionally this relies more on a leap of faith than true etymology. It is interesting that at least some of those places named, dismissed for decades, even centuries, as fictions, have been proved by archaeology to have been occupied by the 'right' class of people in the 'right' time period. Not proof of Arthur, perhaps, but certainly a little more fuel for the truth behind the legend.

During my research, decisions had to be made on where in Britain to anchor this photographic journey through the life and legends of Arthur. Although the tales place him countrywide, only Cornwall is consistently named as the area of his birth and youth. Of those fortresses which began life in the pre-Roman Iron Age and earlier, and which (according to archaeology) were re-fortified in the Dark Ages , the majority most often associated with Arthur or his compatriots are in the West Country. With some reluctance, then, the sites chosen are those in the South and South-West of England. I offer a brief apology to the proponents of Wales, Southern Scotland and Northern England as the home of the 'real' Arthur: perhaps one day, those areas can also be explored in a book like this.

What we hope to do in '**Exploring the Legends & Sites of King Arthur**' is to lead the reader, using photographs of those places as they exist today, through the West Country version of the myths and the histories, from Arthur's birth (and before) to the legends of his death, exploring the Grail Quest and the Knights of the Round Table along the way. The text, as it threads through the photographs, will tell the legends associated with each place (in the voices of several anonymous storytellers), together with information on any archaeological finds made there or how it came to have Arthurian associations. It would be tedious for the reader to plough through all the 'probablies' and 'possiblies' that necessarily come with archaeological discussion and proofs, where nothing is certain: please feel free to insert these where you feel a healthy dose of scepticism is necessary. It may sound as though the 'facts' are written in stone – they are not, and any lack of objectivity is due to my twenty five year obsession with the Arthurian stories. The sites chosen are among the most beautiful in the country and all of them could be visited by the public at the time of writing. Each site has an Ordnance Survey Grid Reference, and the Sheet Number given refers to the 1:50000 Landranger Map Series.

Let me leave the last word to our phantom storyteller:

"Come with me now, my friends, for I invite you to join me on an odyssey through the life and passing of the greatest hero in the long history of Britain. In a time of great darkness, when the wolves of war threatened to devour the land, there came a man who held high a bright flame of hope. His flame stays burning in the hearts of those who hear his story – for whether Arthur Pendragon was flesh and blood or a dream conjured by bards, he has taken on a reality which has grown far beyond his beginnings.
Lords and ladies, I give you Arturus, Rex Quondam, Rexque Futurus – the Once and Future King. For as long as his story continues to be told, Arthur will never die."

Denise Stobie Glastonbury, 1998

The ramparts of South Cadbury hillfort. According to local legend, this is Camelot.

CHAPTER ONE

"BRING US A HOPE…": ARTHUR'S BIRTH AND BEFORE

Dark and feeble as a failing star on a night of grey
Our hopes as the mighty Legions – our brothers and sons
and fathers – sailed away.
On every flank, each coast, each shore
We were beset by the serpents of the sword, the wolves of war. . .
And we, the abandoned ones of Albion
Learned to look to ourselves for freedom, for hope and salvation –
And we prayed that those of the ancient blood would light a flame
That we might follow, or bring us a creation of hope that we might name.

AMESBURY AND WANSDYKE

IN THE DARK DAYS that followed the leaving of the Roman Legions, Britain suffered not only from repeated invasions of Pict, Irish and Saxon, but also from in-fighting amongst the petty chieftains who claimed power over the old tribal lands. Eventually, into this chaos, strode the first players in the Arthurian cycle: **Ambrosius Aurelianus**, 'a Roman whose family had worn the purple' and **Uther**, later called The Pendragon.

Ambrosius became war-leader for the British kings beset by the invaders. One of his camps, the only one which bears a trace of his name today, was centred at 'Ambresbyrig', now **Amesbury** (184: SU 150419), in Wiltshire. His army, which was of considerable size, would have been known as the 'Ambrosiaci' – Ambrosius' men. On wooded ground which is now behind the church of Saints Mary and Melor, he is said to have founded a monastery, and traces of such a building have been found there. Also attributed to Ambrosius is the earthwork known as **Wansdyke** – Wodensdic to the Saxons. This stretches from Bristol in the west to Savernake Forest in the east (with a fifteen mile break in the middle), and was built to protect the land south of its line. Although difficult to man, even with cavalry, it could mark a boundary line between the native British in the south-west and the invading Saxons to the north-east. Certainly it was built by someone with great influence and command in the region.

Woods behind Amesbury Church, Wiltshire, where Ambrosius Aurelianus founded a monastery.

Stonehenge

*When Ambrosius became war-leader, he defeated the High King Vortigern and the Saxons who fought to take over the land of Britain. He wished to build a fitting memorial to his victories, and was advised to send for **Merlin**, 'the cleverest man in the kingdom'. Merlin was received with honour, and suggested that Ambrosius send to Ireland for the 'Dance of the Giants that is in Killare'. After some persuasion, the warlord sent his brother Uther, with 15,000 men, to conquer the king of Ireland and bring back the Giant's Dance. Uther was victorious – but neither he nor all of his men were able to move the great circle of stones. So Merlin constructed ingenious devices and brought the stones down, carrying them to ships and thus to Britain. He reconstructed the Dance of the Giants on Salisbury Plain, close to Amesbury, and it was called **Stonehenge**.*

Soon after, a comet like a fiery dragon appeared in the sky, and Merlin claimed it prophesied Ambrosius' death. He said also that Uther would be King "under the sign of the Dragon", but that Uther's son would be mightiest of all.

STONEHENGE (184: SU 123422) is an awesome monument just off the A303 in Wiltshire. Although permission is needed to enter the stones, even distance cannot detract from the splendour of the construction. It is, of course, many centuries older that Arthur or Ambrosius – some 300 centuries, in fact – but there may be an actual Irish link. Some of the stones have proved to come from the Prescelly Mountains in South Wales, and it is thought that this was an area of Irish settlement. The stones would have been carried to Salisbury Plain by water as well as over land. So a kernel of truth resides in the thought that 'Merlin transported the Giant's Dance over the sea from Ireland' . . .

Left The rising sun at Stonehenge, Wiltshire. Merlin used magic to bring the stones from Ireland.

Below The trilithons of the Giant's Dance, erected to commemmorate Ambrosius' victories.

TREGEARE ROUNDS AND ST DENNIS

*At Uther's coronation feast, he was smitten with desire for the wife of Gorlois, Duke of Cornwall. Despite the risk, he pursued her quite shamelessly, until in the end a furious Gorlois left for his Cornish lands in a storm of scandal. Quite unperturbed, Uther followed, determined not to be thwarted. Perhaps unsurprisingly, war was declared between the two men. And so, with his wife **Ygraine** safely ensconced at **Tintagel**, Gorlois set out to do battle. At a place called Dimilioc, his forces were besieged by the army of Uther, and a long, long wait commenced.*

WE CANNOT find Dimilioc with any certainty today. Six miles/9.6km south of Tintagel is a camp of the Iron Age, which is marked on the map as **Tregeare Rounds** (200: SX 033800) but is more often known as 'Castle Dameliock'. This name seems to be unknown before the nineteenth century, so in light of the next part of our tale, it is possible that it became Dimilioc simply because it is within close riding distance of Tintagel . . .

Twenty miles/32.2km away from Tregeare Rounds, the Domesday Book of 1086 records a manor called 'Dimelihoc'. It was in the parish of **St Dennis** (200:SW 950580), where the modern churchyard wall is a circular one marking an ancient fortification. It is possible, in fact, that St 'Dennis' is a corruption of the British word for fort – 'dinas'. The tradition linking the modern St Dennis with the area of Gorlois' last stand is an old one: both Geoffrey of Monmouth and a later, fifteenth-century writer seem to have this location in mind.

Left *Tregeare Rounds, Cornwall. An Iron Age camp which might have been Dimilioc, where Uther and Gorlois fought.*

Below *St Dennis Church, Cornwall. The churchyard wall marks an ancient fortification.*

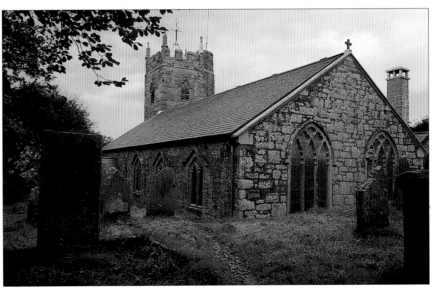

TINTAGEL

We left Gorlois and Uther metaphorically glaring at each other across the battle-lines at Dimilioc. This state of play was broken after a tense week, because Uther could wait no longer. Leaving his commanders in charge, he rode in secret to Tintagel on the wild northern coast, with intentions that could probably not be described as 'honorable'. Merlin, by now established as Uther's adviser and partner-in-crime, used enchantment to produce a glamour, changing Uther into the seeming of Gorlois. Thus disguised, Uther was able to enter the castle and grasp the opportunity to ravish the unwitting Ygraine . . .

TINTAGEL CASTLE (200:SX 048892) rises some 250 ft/77m above the wild Atlantic coast of northern Cornwall. It is now more an island than a promontory, reached by a somewhat precarious path. The castle remains on the island are of the thirteenth and fourteenth centuries, built on the foundations of a fortress a century older. It used to be thought that this castle was in Geoffrey of Monmouth's mind when he made it Gorlois' home (he was writing at the time of the castle's erection), but recent opinion holds that there may have been an older tradition at work.

Above the castle, extensive remains have been found of buildings from the fifth or sixth centuries – Arthur's time. For many decades, this was considered to be a Celtic monastery and thus discounted as a chieftain's stronghold. The current opinion, however, is that these remains are indeed the headquarters of a powerful local lord, and thus the legend is given more credence in the 1990s than it has had for over 100 years.

Uther's absence from Dimilioc had tragic consequences. The stalemate broken, battle ensued and, in the fighting, the real Gorlois was killed. When the defeated army returned to Tintagel with the broken body of their lord, it was to find the Pendragon already in possession of the stronghold and Ygraine – well, let us assume that Ygraine received the greatest shock of all.

*Uther and Ygraine were wed in what seemed, to some, the most indecent haste. The haste was necessary . . . Ygraine was with child. And nine months after the siege of Dimilioc, still close-kept in Tintagel Castle, she gave birth to a boy-child. She named him **Arthur**.*

Far left *Remains of the medieval castle of Tintagel in northern Cornwall. Was the earlier fortress Arthur's birthplace?*

Left *Protected on three sides by the Atlantic, Tintagel still presents a formidable vista - even in sunlight.*

Merlin's Cave, below the windswept cliff path to Tintagel Head. His ghost can still be heard.

MERLIN'S CAVE

BELOW TINTAGEL HEAD and reached by a precarious path, a cave can be seen at low tide. This is **Merlin's Cave** (200:SX 049891), and is said to be haunted by his restless spirit. Guilt, perhaps, at what was done to the deceived new Queen? Perhaps, but there is a purer version of the birth of Arthur, which removes the human element altogether and makes his existence as miraculous as any ancient legend.

Merlin and a companion were descending to the cave, on a night of hideous weather, and from the path witnessed the appearance of a phantom ship shaped like a winged dragon. Though the ship disappeared as quickly as it had come, the waves crashing on the shore by the cave grew mightier and mightier, until the ninth wave brought with it amongst voices and flame a babe, which was swept to Merlin's feet. He plucked the naked child from the foam, crying, "An heir for Uther!" And as he spoke, the sea lashed at him and turned to fire, so that he and the child were surrounded by flame – and then as quickly, wind and water calmed, and the night was full of stars. (After Tennyson, 'Idylls of the King').

However the young Arthur was engendered, we are told that on the night of his birth (which was, presumably, dark, wild and stormy) he was taken swiftly away by Merlin, who was commanded to see to his fostering. He was placed with a knight named Ector, and Uther had no more to do with his upbringing.

CHAPTER TWO

ARTHUR THE YOUTH: WARLORD-IN-WAITING

KELLIWIC: KELLY ROUNDS, BARRAS HEAD AND WILLAPARK

ALTHOUGH IT APPEARS that Uther did not see Arthur again, and Ygraine rarely merits another mention once she had done her duty, all the evidence points to the fact that Arthur's early home remained in the vicinity of Tintagel. Even those storytellers determined to locate him in Wales seem honour-bound to give him a home in indisputably Cornish Kelliwic or Celliwig.

Even after he reached the height of his fame, it seems that Kelliwic remained his seat of power in the South-Western British kingdoms, for the old form of one of the Welsh Triads states:

Arthur's Three Principal Courts (were):
Aberffraw in Wales
and Celliwig in Cornwall
and Penrhyn Rhionydd in the North.

We can put forward some educated guesses for the location of this favourite dwelling of Arthur. **Barras Head (or Nose)** (200:SX 053895) is a headland on the north Cornish coast, in fact the one directly north of Tintagel, although there seems no evidence that it was ever occupied. The next headland up, **Willapark** (200:SX 060898), has Iron Age earthworks across its neck, but no presently known 'Arthurian' remains. Callington, across Bodmin Moor, was a favourite for a long time and then fell out of favour, and Callywith has the right sounding name and woodland ('kellywic' means 'small woodland') but, apparently, no remains. As an eternal optimist, the author is tempted to mutter 'absence of evidence isn't evidence of absence' and move swiftly on to the most likely contender: Castle Killibury or **Kelly Rounds** (200:SX 018737). This hillfort is just east of Wadebridge, and the road on which it is situated continues straight through the old gateway. It has double ramparts, one of which still stands 15 ft / 4.5m high, and is very close to the ancient trade route which crosses the Cornish peninsula.

Kelly Rounds, nr Wadebridge in Cornwall. This may have been Kelliwic, Arthur's childhood home.

ARTHUR'S HUNTING LODGES: ARTHUR'S HALL AND CASTLE-AN-DINAS

IF THIS AREA is indeed the place where Arthur grew up, we can assume that here he learned the arts of all young nobles of his time – hunting, feasting, and fighting. There are two places in Cornwall which are named 'Arthur's Hunting Lodges'.

The first is **Arthur's Hall** (200: SX 130777), stone remains on Bodmin Moor near Garrow Tor. This may be all that remains of a building, or it could be a reservoir of some sort, as it is floored with slabs. We don't know how old it is; there is little dating evidence and it could as well belong to the late Stone Age as to the hunting days of the young Arthur.

The second hunting lodge is **Castle-an-Dinas** (200: SW 945624), near St Columb Major. Nearby Tregoss Moor is said to have been the land where he used to ride. This hillfort is both impressive and strategically placed, but unlike Cadbury Castle and Castle Dore, archaeology has failed to find evidence that it was occupied later than the Roman invasion.

Left *Arthur's Hall on lonely Bodmin Moor. It may have been a hunting lodge. dating from the Dark Ages.*

Below *Castle-an-Dinas, an Iron Age hillfort which might have housed the young Arthur on hunting expeditions.*

DUNSTER, BAT'S CASTLE, CARHAMPTON AND CADBURY-CONGRESBURY

No WARRIOR, however much natural aptitude he may have, comes from nowhere to command. He must train, and learn, and hone his skills, and he must first have a superior officer. We first hear of Arthur the warrior as a junior officer to **Cadwy ap Geraint**, a prince of Dumnonia.

The 'Life of Saint Carannog' tells us that the saint had a floating altar, which he set adrift in the Bristol Channel. He vowed to preach wherever it landed. Eventually, he traced its landing place to Dindraethou (or Dindraithov) on the north Somerset coast, Somerset at that time being part of the vast south-western kingdom of Dumnonia. But when he arrived there, the altar was nowhere to be found. Close by, he was told, Prince Cadwy's junior colleague was attempting to fight a dragon which was terrorising the people of Carrum. The warrior, one Arthur, told the saint that he certainly did know where the altar could be found – but he would only give up the information if Carannog aided him in ridding the land of the troublesome dragon. Despite the fact that this attitude failed to show proper respect for the church, Carannog (in the best saintly style) promptly tamed the creature and freed Carrum from danger.

Then Arthur revealed that it was he who had found the altar, and he had been trying to use it as a table. It was useless for the purpose, for everything he placed upon it was promptly hurled off. In gratitude for Carannog's help, Arthur said he could settle at Carrum and preach there for as long as he wished.

Dindraethou has been identified as **Dunster** (181: SS 992435) in Somerset. Although the castle there is medieval, there is no reason to suppose that a fifth century prince and his joint (if junior) ruler did not have headquarters there. Also nearby is **Bat's Castle Hillfort** (181: SS 988421), which could also have been refortified and used as a centre for Cadwy and Arthur, although archaeological evidence is lacking for this.

Carrum, with its troublesome serpent, is nearby **Carhampton** (181: ST 009427), and land which once belonged to its church is supposed to be that granted to Carannog by Arthur.

Cadwy, the prince of the area, could well be the person for whom Caddanbyrig, or Cadbury, was named. If this is so, then it is more than likely that when Arthur took over as warleader, he also took over the forts held by the prince. Further north in Somerset is another Cadbury, **Cadbury-Congresbury** (182: ST 440650), which may have been part of the same chain.

Far left *Dunster beach in north Somerset, where St Carranog's floating altar came to rest.*

ST JULITTA'S WELL

It is said that Uther Pendragon reigned for a further fifteen years after the birth of his famous son, and there is more than one version of his death. All begin by telling us that Britain suffered greatly throughout Uther's reign from constant attacks by both Saxons and Scots (Irish). Uther was ill for a long time before his death, and appointed Lot of Lothian as warleader. As often as Lot won a victory, the enemy returned, and 'almost all the island was laid waste': Then Uther became enraged, and called all his captains to him, vowing that he would lead the army himself. And, carried on a litter, this he did, and after a long fight the British were victorious.

Below *Bat's Castle hillfort, near Dunster. This could be Cadwy's fort of Dindraethou.*

The myth now takes on three forms:

The king's illness worsened, weakened as he was by the mighty effort of the Saxon war. Eventually, Merlin came to him and asked him to acknowledge Arthur as his son and the new king. This he did, and soon afterwards he died, and was buried in the Giant's Dance beside his brother Ambrosius.

Both of the remaining stories say that Uther was poisoned, and only the place of this ignominious act differs:

In Verulamium (St Alban's), there was a spring of the purest water which the king used to drink when his illness made it impossible for him to take any other sustenance. One dark night, Saxon traitors crept to the spring and poisoned it, so that all the water was infected. When the King drank of the spring, he died immediately. (After Geoffrey of Monmouth)

The other location for Uther's fatal betrayal was Tintagel, and specifically, the water of the well of **St Julitta** (200: SX 048892) or Ulette. This is one of three wells on the 'island', and there are the remains of a chapel close by. A local tradition states that 'Gottlouis' himself dedicated the chapel to St Ulette, and that Uther, visiting from Winchester, was poisoned here in the year 515.

Below *Carhampton Church, near Dunster. This is Carrum, where Arthur gave land to St Carranog.*

Right *Cadbury-Congresbury hillfort, near Bristol. It may have been named after Cadwy, Arthur's commander.*

CHAPTER THREE

ARTHUR PENDRAGON: WARRIOR AND SCOURGE OF THE SAXONS

Who will carry Britain's banner　　　　*One whose wyrd is brilliant as*
The standard of the Dragon crimson　　*A comet's tail in darkest night-time -*
Who will lead the land to victory?　　*Aye, there is one whose name will shine*
Divided land, the kings are warring　　*Ever brighter than the stars!*
Who will wear the crown?　　　　　*Uther's gone, but night is ending*
For Uther is dying . . .　　　　　　*See the flame flare high*
Uther Pendragon, dying!　　　　　*Arthur is waking . . .*

Arthur Pendragon, rising!
Arthur ab Uther, Arthur Pendragon, all hail!
(Denise Stobie & Val Joice, 1982)

FROM THIS POINT ON, Arthur's 'reign' can be divided neatly into three parts: his campaigns against Britain's enemies (Pict, Saxon, Irish and, in one Cornish tradition, red-haired Danes), culminating in the glorious victory at Mount Badon; the twenty years of peace following Badon, where we can place the chivalrous romances, the Grail Quest and the Tristan & Yseult love story; and finally, the 'strife of Camlan where Arthur and Medraut fell', and all the myths about the fate of the great leader and his sword, Caliburn.

The medieval legends, which are the best known cycle of traditions, concentrate on the Round Table and the romances. It is the earlier chronicle of Nennius which provides us with a roll of honour commemorating Arthur's 'real' victories. Nennius lists twelve battles, none of which we can now locate with any certainty. They range from Scotland to the south-west of England.

The first battle was 'at the mouth of the river which is called Glein', and suggested sites for this are in Lincolnshire and Northumberland. The second, third, fourth and fifth were beside a 'river which is called Dubglas and is in the region Linnuis'.

RIVER DIVELISH AND DEVIL'S BROOK

THE FACT that four battles took place on the Dubglas points to a major offensive (probably Saxon), and some modern historians dismiss a south-western location because, as far as we know, the Saxons hadn't ranged so far west at that time. As the boundaries of evidence are being shifted all the time, however, the author claims the right to place Dubglas firmly in Dorset, as others have suggested.

The first Dorset river which could be the Dubglas is the **River Divelish** (194: ST 795145), near Sturminster Newton and feeding into the River Stour. The second is the **Devil's Brook** (194: SY 779983), flowing from a source near Bulbarrow southward into the Piddle (or Trent). A nearby village is Dewlish. All three of these modern names are versions of the original Dubglas – meaning 'black water'. If we play a little with Nennius' extra information 'in the region Linnuis' – although we're relying on a possible spelling mistake by a nameless scribe – we can take it further.

There are a lot of 'ifs' in the argument.

Ilchester in Somerset was known during the Roman occupation as Lindinis. The people of the surrounding area would have been the Lindinienses, and the region itself, Lininuis. If their lands stretched 20 miles/30km further west and if a scribe missed out a single letter 'i' when copying the manuscript, then the Divelish or Devil's Brook becomes the Dubglas. . .

Ilchester was occupied in the Arthurian period and was a junction for several major Roman roads, including the Fosse Way. It is only a few miles from the Arthurian stronghold of Cadbury.

See Arthur's warband march down from their fortress, banners flying, spearheads shining. See them, hear them march through Lindinis, on their way to defeat the upstart Saxon raiders who have been terrorising the land – Arthur's land – miles west of their own country . . . look well, look hard . . .

That's how legends are born, and why history can be deadly dull in comparison.

Left *The River Divelish, near Sturminster Newton, Dorset. 'Divelish' is a version of 'Dubglas'.*

Right *The Devil's Brook, near Dewlish, Dorset. Was this the site of four battles 'beside the river called Dubglas'?*

ST BRIDE'S MOUND AND WELL, BECKERY

THE NEXT LISTED BATTLES after Dubglas take place elsewhere in Britain. Arthur's warband relied on swift-moving cavalry for their strength, and as well as giving them speed of attack, it allowed them to battle over a far-ranging area, even as far north as the Forest of Caledonia in Scotland and Chester near the (modern) Welsh border. Although one of his battles, at Castle Guinnion, took place at some unknown site, we are told that here he carried the image of the Virgin on his shield, replacing the earlier red dragon. It could be that this shield device was inspired by a vision he had at Beckery, in Avalon, of the Virgin and Christ-Child. This is told in a fourteenth century tale by John of Glastonbury:

On Wirral (Wearyall) Hill, in Glastonbury, stood in the time of Arthur a convent dedicated to St Peter, which the Pendragon often visited. One night, he dreamed an angel commanded him to go, with the coming of dawn, to the little church of St Mary Magdalene at Beckery. Bewildered but obedient, he did so. On entering the chapel, he beheld the Blessed Virgin Mary and her infant Son. Marvelling, Arthur watched a wondrous vision, as the child was slaughtered and miraculously made whole again. Arthur vowed then that Mary would be his guiding principle in life.

There have been no relevant finds on Wearyall Hill in Glastonbury, so we cannot prove the existence of a 'convent' there. Excavations in the 1960s, however, do prove the existence of a small chapel, dedicated to Mary Magdalene, on a mound above the high water line of the Somerset Levels. Now called **St Bride's Mound** (182: ST485384) after the Irish saint who allegedly stayed there for a while, it is at present under shoulder-high nettles on private land. The Mound is in an area called Beckery, now a suburb of Glastonbury but once a small, separate village.

Not far from the site of this ancient chapel, beside a footpath along the River Brue, is a stone which marks **St Bride's Well**. It is now about 360ft/100m from its original site. This well was presumably once a natural spring, and we know from nineteenth and early twentieth century accounts that its waters were murky but formed a definite pool. A cup, considered by some to be the Grail itself, was found there in 1906; it had been placed there by a Dr Goodchild in 1898, who had found it and a 'dish' in Italy a few years earlier. It is a long and fascinating spiritual tale, ably and fully recounted in Patrick Benham's book '*The Avalonians*' (Gothic Image Publications, 1993).

This stone marks the site of St Bride's Well, near Glastonbury. Here, Arthur had a vision of the Virgin Mary.

Badbury Rings, Dorset, a hillfort which stands near a Roman road.

BADBURY RINGS, LITTLE SOLSBURY HILL, BATHAMPTON DOWN AND LIDDINGTON CASTLE

The clash of steel rose in the morning
And brave the deeds I tell -
As heroes rode to save this land
And to rid us of its hell.
Our foes held strong, with their shields afire -
But could not hope to stand
As warriors brave sent them to their graves
And won freedom for this land!

Victory, victory! Lords raise up your cry
For victory, sweet victory, we raise our glasses high!

IT IS THE LAST and greatest of the twelve battles that we must seek now, because 'the twelfth battle was the seige of Mount Badon, in which 960 men fell in one day from one charge of Arthur, and no-one overthrew them except himself alone'. One thing is certain: however vague and misty the truth behind Arthur, someone led the British to a masterful victory at 'Mons Badonicus'. He prevented the Saxon settlers from attempting to take the British west for at least twenty years, a momentous achievement.

There are three places which might be Badon. The furthest west is **Badbury Rings** (195: ST 964030) in Dorset. This hillfort stands about 100 ft/31m high, between Blandford and Wimborne, beside an old Roman road. The name is right, but the place . . .?

If we come eastward, closer to the Saxon lands, we find Bath (or better, 'Baddan', pronounced Bath-an), the Saxon name for a pre-Roman holy spring and Roman Spa town. Outside the Roman city walls lie to one side **Little Solsbury Hill** (172: ST 768679) and, to the other, **Bathampton Down** (172: ST 776647), where the university is now. Both hills have earthworks. Both are strategically important. And Bath itself was vital to Saxon expansion plans, as their next real offensive in 577 AD shows. Mount Badon? It is difficult now to imagine two great armies facing each other in a siege here, for the motorway and the suburbs intrude too much, but remove the modern trappings and one can picture the campfires and hear the sounds of impending war . . .

Eastward again, until we reach the prehistoric track now called the Ridgeway. On this ancient highway, just outside Swindon, is a village named by the Saxons 'Baddanbyrig', and now called Badbury. Nearby is the hillfort of **Liddington Castle** (174: SU 208796). Its Iron Age ramparts were partially re-fortified at the time of Arthur, and it overlooks a Roman

Little Solsbury Hill, outside Bath. Another contender for the site of the battle of Badon.

road which is on the most direct route a Saxon army would have taken from the Thames valley. By following the river valley and then the old track, they would have turned west through a pass in the hills and joined the Roman road on their march into Dumnonia. Liddington protects the pass.

See the armies surrounding the hill, and the defenders looking down and waiting for the horn to sound the charge . . . hear the snort of the horses in the lines, the rhythmic song of stone on metal as swords are honed, the catcalls and insults between Briton and Saxon . . . and with the dawn, the call goes up and with a mighty roar warrior meets warrior and sword clashes on sword . . .

No-one now knows who besieged whom, and in the light of Arthur's victory, it simply doesn't matter. Suffice it to say that at Badon, our Pendragon Warlord stopped the enemy advance and secured the bright freedom of the British for the next two decades.

Below *Bathampton Down, outside Bath. The University of Bath stands here now.*

Right *Liddington Castle, Wiltshire, stands proud above the ancient Ridgeway.*

ZENNOR, ZENNOR HEAD, CARN VELLAN AND TREREEN DINAS

BEFORE LEAVING Arthur the warrior, another battle should be mentioned although it doesn't feature in any 'historical' document. Instead, it's an Arthurian tradition firmly attached to the most western part of Cornwall.

It is said by those still living between St Ives and Land's End that, many years ago, a great host of red-haired men – Danes, they say – landed at Whitesand Bay. These ferocious Vikings terrorised the land all around, until finally, the great High King Arthur was summoned from Camelot to fight the invaders. He came to Zennor and, joined by four Cornish kings, marched from Madron to Zennor Head, where they dined together off a flat rock. Rested and fed, the combined armies marched to Vellan and fought the Danes. Fierce was the fighting and loud were the cries, but the British led by Arthur won the day, and the Danes were driven into the sea. They had been ashore for so long, however, that birds had nested in the rigging of their ships and they had begotten many a red-haired infant on the local women. For many generations, red-headed families could be found in the area, but the other country folk were wary of them for their ancestry, and did not like to marry them.

Zennor (203: SW 454385) and **Zennor Head** (203: SW 450393), where the British armies joined forces and ate a leisurely meal, are on the South West Coastal Path, near Pendeen. **Carn Vellan**

Left *Zennor, Cornwall, where Arthur met four Cornish kings.*

Below *Zennor Head, with Trereen Dinas in the distance.*

(203: SW369344), near where the battle took place, is near the B3306 just west of Pendeen. **Trereen Dinas** (203: SW 432387) is an Iron Age promontory fort on Gurnard's Head, with three ramparts still visible, and even today can only be approached by footpath. Although no Arthurian traces have been found, the tradition calls it his castle for the duration of this campaign.

Below *Carn Vellan, where Arthur and his companions faced the Danes.*

Below *The remains of old tin mines stand on the site of one of Arthur's Cornish battles.*

Right *Trereen Dinas, in the distance, is an Iron Age promontory fort, defended by the ocean.*

CHAPTER FOUR

CAMELOT AND THE KNIGHTS OF THE ROUND TABLE

Where is bright Camelot? That place where Arthur and his knights feasted at the Table Round, where Guinevere lit the hall with her radiant beauty, where chivalry flourished in the years of peace after the glorious victory of Badon . . . where are they now?

Camelot was never a spired castle. Imagine instead a fortified hilltop, with giant banks and ditches encircling the slopes. Atop the highest bank is a stockade of logs – small trees, perhaps – several feet high, stretching around the entire perimeter of the hill. Soldiers man a walkway behind the walls. A fine double gateway opens at the head of a wide, cobbled road, guarded by men in iron and leather helmets, armed with small-headed spears and whitewashed round shields, red cloaks slung around their shoulders over leather armour and, in a few lucky cases, mail shirts. Mail is hideously expensive, and few warriors can afford it. Many a mail shirt has been stolen from dead Saxons; the dead don't need them and the living must be armoured somehow. As you approach the gate, you can see beyond, where the land slopes up to the small plateau which seems higher than the stockade itself. There stands a long, low hall, its roof thatched, its plaster-and-wattle walls newly smoothed. Smoke curls lazily from the roof-holes. Although you have seen other halls like it, this is the finest, this is the richest. You pass through the gate, and find that many thatched buildings – some round, some rectangular – stretch across the entire hilltop. A great chieftain must live here, for on this one hill must be housed more people than you have ever imagined in your life. It's like a city of the Romans, which your grandsire has described on long winter evenings. You look around you, and you whisper, "Camelot?"

SOUTH CADBURY CASTLE

THERE HAVE been several suggestions for the location of Camelot, including Caerleon and Chester. But in recent years only one place has become widely accepted as the home or headquarters of an 'Arthur-type figure': **Cadbury Castle** (183: ST 628252), between the little Somerset villages of South Cadbury and Sutton Montis. It is first mentioned as Arthur's Camelot by John Leland in 1542, and seems to have been a strong local tradition at that time. The nearby villages of West and Queen Camel may have added strength to the claim.

The impressive hill stands some 500ft/152m above sea level and the surrounding land, and the innermost defensive rampart surrounds an area of about 18 acres/7 hectares. Excavation has shown that it has been occupied as a defended site since Neolithic times, some 5000 years, with its heyday just before the Roman Conquest, in about 45AD. The most important evidence, however, came from layers closer to the surface – and therefore, closer in time to us.

Cadbury was massively re-fortified in the late fifth or early sixth century, by a person of great importance. He must have had a huge retinue to need so much space – the entire, windswept hilltop is enclosed – and he must have had, or been able to acquire, the resources to rebuild on a grand scale. The best approach is from the village of South Cadbury, up a hedge-lined path to a gap in the ramparts. This gap is all that remains of one of the lesser gateways. The opposite corner of the enclosure shows a wider but flatter gap: the main gate, just a hollowed out path now, but once a two-storey square gateway with two sets of massive double doors, and a ten foot wide road winding down towards what is now Sutton Montis. The stonework which is exposed around the inner bank is late Saxon.

South Cadbury Castle, Somerset, was refortified in Arthurian times. Fragments of pottery show that he and his 'court', for want of a better term, were able to import goods from the Mediterranean, like oil and wine. Cadbury was not the home of a peasant farmer.

KING ARTHUR'S CAUSEWAY, SPRING AND WELL

On winter nights, when the moon is high, wait by the track at Camelot. Though nothing catches your eye except shade and moon shadows, you may hear them ride by: Arthur and his men, hoofbeats clattering, with their horns and their hounds on their way to hunt.

At night, I hear you ask? Aye, at night, for Arthur is not only the king under the hill, but in this land he leads a different kind of hunt – a wild, wild hunt. He calls to his red-eyed hounds as the moonlight silvers the sky, for tonight, my lads, the hunters ride. Bar your doors and shutters tight, for when the Wild Hunt rides all the world will freeze and you'll have no place left to run . . .

Ah child, whisper soft. Best not to ask what Arthur's prey might be.

Left *Arthur's Well, on the path which once led to the north-east gate of the fortress.*

Below *Sutton Montis Church, where Arthur and his knights still drink from the ancient well.*

But Arthur does not always ride so wild from Camallate. I hear tell that on a certain night of the year, he and his horsemen ride over the hilltop from Arthur's palace, pass two by two through the ancient gate, and wend their way down their ancient road to drink from the spring by the new church. Some say this happens not every year, but every seven, and it may be on Midsummer Eve, or Midsummer Night, or Christmas Eve. If the night is full of mist, or the moon's face is wrong, then you will only hear their hoofbeats and the jingle of their harness.

I have neither seen nor heard them, though a friend of mine once knew someone who found a silver horseshoe on the track. Perhaps, my friends, you should go out on all these nights, and seek them for yourself!

KING ARTHUR'S HUNTING CAUSEWAY follows the line of an old (possibly ancient) track which runs from Cadbury towards Glastonbury. It is not really discernible now, probably due to the draining of the Somerset levels and subsequent rise of the land.

At the left-hand side of the path which climbs the hill from South Cadbury village is a well, known as **King Arthur's Well**. Over the hill and down into Sutton Montis, we find the tradition of **King Arthur's Spring** (183: ST 624248) beside the church, although the spring itself also seems to have been lost in recent times. Obviously, the knights and their lord were not short of watering places.

A little way from Cadbury, on the A371 between Castle Cary and Shepton Mallet, you can cross **Arthur's Bridge** (183: ST 638359) over the River Alham. The sign is very modern, and it may be that both bridge and Arthurian association are too.

Arthur's Bridge, over the River Alham north of Cadbury. Both bridge and sign are modern.

THE ROUND TABLE, WINCHESTER

What a dowry! It took fourteen men to haul that blasted table into Camelot when my lady Gwenhwyfar (oh all right, then, Guinevere) brought it to her marriage with the Lord Arthur. Whether it was Merlin's idea, or her father's, or her own, it was a strange sort of gift.

They say that the Round Table was an idea as much as it was a piece of furniture. No knight could claim himself to be better than another, for there was no 'high' table or 'low' table, simply the Table Round, where all were equal. There was a seat for every knight, and his name was marked at his place. Of course, the King's seat was a bit 'higher' – after all, he was the King. Oh yes, and there was the Perilous Seat, next to the King. Strange that it remained empty for many a year.

I thought they called it 'perilous' because the maid who served Arthur was dreadfully clumsy, and you stood to get wine or gravy or Merlin knew what else in your lap if you sat there – but more learned people than me said the chair was waiting for the most perfect knight to claim his place. Anyone else would die. Mind you, once Galahad proved himself perfect by remaining alive once he sat there, it put a bit of a damper on the idea of equality. . .

This Round Table, in Castle Hall, Winchester, is a famous medieval forgery.

THE FAMOUS ROUND TABLE is a forgery. It has no Arthurian history, although as a concept it remains impressive. It hangs on the wall in Castle Hall, **Winchester** (185: SU 480295). Recent testing using archaeological dating methods show that it was probably made in the reign of Edward I of England (1272-1307). It is first mentioned in 1450, when it was generally accepted as the 'real' Table used by Arthur and his knights. It was re-painted, much as it appears now, in 1522 during the early reign of Henry VIII, and it is his portrait painted at the King's seat. The emblem in the centre is the Tudor Rose.

The Round Table might well have been a meeting place rather than a piece of furniture, it might have been a circular hillfort like Tregeare Rounds or Castle Dore, or a Roman amphitheatre such as still exists at Caerleon in Wales.

DINGEREIN CASTLE, VERYAN BEACON AND PORTCHESTER

THESE PLACES, with the exception of Portchester, appear to have been named for Gereint, the husband of Enid and Knight of the Round Table. He appears to have been a ruler in his own right in Cornwall – perhaps one of the four Cornish kings called upon by Arthur to fight the Danes around Zennor and Carn Vellan.

When Gereint died, it is said that his body was placed in a golden boat with silver oars, and he was rowed across Gerrans Bay. He was buried in a huge mound, and many mourned his passing. This mound is probably meant to be **Veryan Beacon** (204: SW 913387), a prehistoric burial mound in existence long before Gereint or Arthur's time, or perhaps **Dingerein** (204: SW 882375) nearby, a name meaning 'Gereint's Fort'.

An early Welsh poem mentions both Gereint and 'Arthur's men' fighting a battle at a place called Llongborth. Although this may be Langport in Somerset, it is thought more likely to be **Portchester** in Hampshire (196: SU 965030), where there is an existing Roman tower, one of the Saxon Shore forts. The poem runs:

In Llongborth I saw the clash of swords
Men in terror, bloody heads
Before Gereint the Great, his father's son

In Llongborth I saw Arthur's
Brave men who cut with steel -
The Emperor, ruler of our labour

One version of this Welsh elegy claims that Gereint was killed in the battle, and the Anglo-Saxon Chronicle records the death of a very high-ranking young Briton during a Saxon raid at Portchester in around 500AD – very close to the time of Badon.

Below *Brent Knoll stands beside the M5 in Somerset. It was once an island known as the Hill of Frogs.*

BRENT KNOLL

The newest of the knights of the Round Table was named Yder. Eager to prove himself, he begged Arthur to give him a task worthy of his new rank. So Arthur told him of three giants who were terrorising the neighbourhood of Mons Ranarus – the Hill of the Frogs. Enthusiastic and brave, determined to earn honour in his own right, Yder galloped ahead of those who rode with him. Though Arthur and his companions thought Yder rash and impetuous, the Pendragon let him go. "He must learn," was all Arthur would say, and he slowed their pursuit so that Yder fought alone.

Deeply did Arthur regret this, for when he and his men reached the hill they found the three giants slain, and Yder dying beside them. He had fought mightily, but did not have the strength to survive the battle.

In penance, Arthur took Yder's broken body to Glastonbury for burial, and gave the land around the Hill of the Frogs to the monks in payment for prayers for the young knight's soul.

BRENT KNOLL (182: ST 341510) is a hill in Somerset, standing beside the M5. It is an impressive hillfort, rising 450 ft/137.5m above the Somerset Levels. There is no sign today of the frogs which gave it its Latin name, but finds have been made which link it to Arthurian times. There is a theory that Brent Knoll was one of a line of beacons which linked Cadbury, Glastonbury Tor, Brent Knoll and Dinas Powys in south-east Wales, close to the Bristol Channel. The lines of visibility are very clear.

GLASTONBURY, PONTER'S BALL AND ITS SURROUNDINGS

The oldest story connecting Arthur and Glastonbury is this:

Melwas, king of the Summer Land or Gwlad yr Haf, desired Arthur's lady Gwenhwyfar. When she spurned his advances, he abducted her from Camelot, and rode off with her to his fortress at Ynis Witrin, which we now call Glastonbury. Enraged, Arthur pursued them with his forces brought from Dumnonia, but in those days Ynis Witrin was an island, surrounded on all sides by water and marsh, and Arthur's great force could not reach the fortress on the hill. Only a few men were able to pass, and the fighting was terrible to see.

Finally, after many days, the abbot of the great church below the Tor came with Saint Gildas, a monk there, to arrange a treaty between the two lords and allow Gwenhwyfar to be returned to her husband. Eventually, the warring men agreed terms, and vowed to keep peace between them. The vows were made in the Old Church of St Mary, the most ancient church in Britain, and Arthur and his wife were reunited in the shadow of the Tor.

LATER VERSIONS of this story change the name of Melwas to Meleagraunce, make Guinevere's rescuer Lancelot, and move the whole story to Lambeth. One of the medieval versions, however, has interesting implications if we leave the setting at Glastonbury. It says that:

Melwas' Castle was on an island, and to this island there were only two bridges: the Sword Bridge, which was composed of a finely wrought and wondrously strong blade of steel which reached from bank to bank; and the Underwater Bridge, which was treacherous and stood as far below the surface of the water as it was above the river bed. The slightest false step from either of these bridges would send a man to his death in the maelstrom.

In the fifth and sixth centuries, Glastonbury was surrounded by water and there were only two land approaches: one from the south-east, where the A361 runs now to Shepton Mallet, and one via a very narrow causeway from the south-west, now the A39 approach from Street. The first approach would have been very well-defended, as it leads almost directly to the foot of the Tor, and an earthwork known as **Ponter's Ball** (182: ST 534379) crosses this line. The causeway, on the other hand, would have been narrow and treacherous, and easily defended by a small force of men. With marsh and water on either side, it would have been difficult to cross, and might well have been the inspiration for the 'Sword Bridge' of the later tale, which was best crossed barefoot.

Ponter's Ball, beside the A361 on the way to Glastonbury. It is a bank and ditch of uncertain date.

The only other way to enter Glastonbury at this time was by water, and the currents would have been well known to the inhabitants of the area. The strongest of these currents was likely to have been the River Brue, which again would have taken a force of men almost to the foot of Melwas' hilltop fortress. At the time, the Brue would have been a strong (if sluggish) current not visible from the surface – perhaps even 'as far below the surface as it was above the river bed'. This could be the 'Underwater Bridge' risked by another would-be rescuer in the medieval romance.

Did Melwas have a castle on **Glastonbury Tor** (182: ST 512386)? Excavations of the summit have found both monastic and secular remains from approximately the correct period. It is very possible that there was indeed a small fortress or signal station here, and there is no reason to suppose that its lord holder was not Melwas, King of the Summer Lands.

We will return to Glastonbury in later tales . . .

Glastonbury Tor on a frosty day. In Arthur's time it was called Ynis Witrin, which means Island of Glass. There may have been a chieftain's fortress where the tower now stands.

CASTLE DORE

BEFORE WE LEAVE Arthur's men, we must tell the story of one of the better of Arthur's knights, who was born in Lyonesse and tragically fell in love (through misplaced sorcery) with his uncle's beautiful second wife. The knight was called Tristan, the uncle was King Mark of Cornwall and the girl, Yseult.

Tristan of Lyonesse was known as a brave and skilful fighter and a fine harpist. When Mark of Cornwall, Tristan's uncle, decided to make a powerful second marriage with the daughter of an Irish king, it was Tristan who was sent to make suit and escort the princess back to Cornwall.

As such marriages of convenience were common in those days, the Irish king was proud to give his daughter's hand in marriage to the Cornish King. But because Mark was ageing, and Yseult a mere girl, her mother worried that the marriage may not be happy. So she created a potion and gave it to Yseult's servant Brangwain, with the grave warning that none should drink it except Mark and his new young queen. It was a powerful love philtre, and whoever drunk it would fall in love for life and all eternity, and the spell could never be broken.

On the voyage back to Cornwall, Tristan and Yseult became very close, for Brangwain was dreadfully seasick and could not chaperone them as she should. One afternoon, when Tristan sought more wine, he found the bottle containing the potion in the cabin of the sleeping Brangwain. Both he and Yseult drained its contents, not knowing what would befall, and it seemed suddenly to each of them that the other glowed with an inner light, and on that day their tragic love was born.

Castle Dore (200: SX 103548) is said to be the home of Mark, also known as Cunomorus. It is a double-ramparted Iron Age hillfort, strategically placed on the ancient trade route across the Cornish peninsula, and was re-fortified during the fifth and sixth centuries. The ramparts still stand some 6-7 ft/2m high. Excavations have uncovered the remains of two halls, one of which was much larger than Arthur's Palace at Cadbury, the other being approximately the same size. An extension to the hall has been interpreted as a Lady's Bower. Not all of the interior has been excavated, nor has the outer gate which may well have been defended by a similar gatehouse to that found at Cadbury. A cobbled road led into the interior.

There is a place called Kilmarth approximately 1.5miles/2.4km away, a name meaning 'Mark's Retreat'.

Recent work has caused doubt to be placed on the 'Arthurian' occupation of Castle Dore, but the tradition is so firmly entrenched in the area there seems no reason to ignore it.

Castle Dore, near Fowey, Cornwall, is said to be the site of King Mark's Castle.

LANTYAN WOOD AND ST SAMPSON-IN-GOLANT

THE EARLY TRISTAN ROMANCES claim that Mark's Palace was in the area of Lancien. In the Middle Ages, Castle Dore was in an administrative area known as the manor of Lantyan-in-Golant, and even today, the name of the manor is preserved in a nearby farm known as Lantyne. This woodland, **Lantyan Wood** (200: SX 110570), runs between the ancient Saints Way and the Fowey estuary, very close to the ancient monastery site of St Sampson.

Yseult came with an escort of her husband's men along the paved road to the monastery church of St Sampson, and presented to the monastery a fine gift. This gift was a silk robe embroidered in gold, and at the time I heard the tale told (many years later), it was still being used as a chasuble once a year, on their anniversary feast.

The church of **St Sampson-in-Golant** (200: SX 121551) as it now stands was dedicated in 1509, but to the left hand side of the porch is an ancient well which would have been visited – perhaps even drunk from – by the royal visitor, Queen Yseult of Cornwall.

Above *The 16th century church of St Sampson-in-Golant, built over an ancient monastery visited by Queen Yseult.*

Left *Lantyan Wood, known as Lancien to Tristan and Yseult. The Saint's Way, an ancient pilgrim's route, is just out of sight on the left of the picture.*

CHAPEL POINT AND ROCHE ROCK

Although Tristan and the queen tried to resist the magic that was wrought betweeen them, it soon became impossible to resist. They made love in secret, but one day were discovered, and Mark's fury knew no bounds.

Now some tell us that Mark kept Yseult with him, in order that she should suffer for her treason, but exiled Tristan from his lands. Others say that the lovers fled together, and were pursued for many a day. Whatever the truth of it, it so happened that Tristan remained in the land of Cornwall, and eventually sought shelter in the hermitage of Ogrin, a holy man of those parts. But Mark's soldiers, relentless in the chase, found him there and made to kill him. Contrite and repentant, Tristan begged them to let him make confession one last time, and to pray before the altar of the chapel. This they allowed him, knowing that he could not escape them.

He prayed, aye, but for deliverance, not absolution. And when the soldiers suspected that all was not as it should be, and crashed back the doors of the chapel, they found Tristan poised to leap from the window to the ground many feet below. He turned and looked at them over his shoulder, and laughed wildly, mocking them. Then as the captain leapt forward to sieze him he leapt with a mighty yell, and disappeared from view. Certain that he would die on the rocks below they crowded around the window, in time to see Tristan wave at them with a jaunty air, and flee into the darkness away from their hounds.

Chapel Point, near Mevagissey in southern Cornwall. It is thought to be the site of Tristan's Leap, where the hero escaped his pursuers.

Two sites lay claim to be the location of 'Tristan's Leap', an heroic escape worthy of the old sagas.

Chapel Point (204: SX 039433), near to Mevagissey, has been long considered to be the location of the leap, although it seems to be some distance from other events. One must remember, of course, that Tristan was trying to escape, so it would make little sense for him to have remained close to home. The poet Beroul, who seems to have known the area quite well, claims that the local people of the area still called the place 'Tristan's Leap' in his time (twelfth century).

The other location for the escape is the chapel of the hermit Ogrin, and **Roche Rock** (200: SW 991595), 5 miles/8km north of St Austell, was such a hermitage. The still impressive chapel remains date from the fifteenth century, but tradition claims a hermitage from the days of early Christianity.

Below and inset Roche Rock and the remains of a 15th century chapel, perhaps the hermitage of Ogrin.

THE TRISTAN STONE

We are told that Tristan remined in exile for many years, never losing the love he felt for Yseult, even though he married. Far from Lancien, Mark's homeland, he was mortally wounded and lay close to death. He knew that only Yseult could save him, and he sent a ship for her, asking the captain to raise a white sail on his return if Yseult was with him, and a black sail if she was not. But Tristan's wife was sick with jealousy, and when she saw the ship on the horizon, she told the weak Tristan that the sail was black, a lie that killed him.

So when Yseult came there, she found her beloved dead only a few minutes and still warm, and in her despair, she too died. They were buried side by side, and the trees that grew from their graves reached towards each other and grew together, so that they were together in death as they had never been in life.

THE **TRISTAN STONE** (200: SX 112521) is a 7ft/2m high memorial stone which has been moved several times since its erection some time in the sixth century. It now stands near crossroads on the road from Castle Dore to Fowey, and is easily missed. Its original location is not known, but it is assumed to be closer to the Castle than it is now.

The inscription on the stone, now much weathered, reads 'DRUSTANUS HIC IACET CUNOMORI FILIUS'. Translated, this means 'Here lies Drustanus, son of Cunomorus'. Drustanus is a form of the name Tristan. We know that a historically authenticated Cunomorus (Kynvawr or Kynvarch in British) ruled this area and also had influence in Brittany at this time. A poet tells us that he was known as Marcus Cunomorus; whether this is to link the stone with the legend or actually true, we now have no way of knowing.

There is one slight problem here, for in the romances it is made very clear that Tristan was Mark's nephew, not his son. Of course, propriety may have made the change necessary as falling in love with one's stepmother was probably something of a taboo in the Middle Ages.

Nevertheless, the location of so many sites in such a relatively small area means that we cannot dismiss the Tristan stories at all – nor should we wish to.

The Tristan Stone, a 6th century memorial stone near Fowey, Cornwall which lends truth to a myth.

CHAPTER FIVE

SEEKING THE HOLY GRAIL

ST NECHTAN'S GLEN AND KIEVE

For many years, the Fellowship of the Round Table remained strong, but the knights grew restless for lack of excitement. One year, at Pentecost, Arthur and Gwenhwyfar were holding their annual feast, and all the knights were present. Suddenly, the doors of the Great Hall flew open, and the revellers were astonished to see a woman enter, bearing in her hands a chalice covered with a veil of white samite. She passed among the knights and their ladies, and wherever she passed, their plates were filled with whatever food they most enjoyed. Then she left, as suddenly and as silently as she had arrived.

People leapt to their feet, demanding to know what this strange vision had been. No-one could agree on a description of the woman, but all knew that the cup she carried was a great and wonderful thing, which had shone with a light of its own, though none had seen it clearly. This, they thought, must have been the Holy Grail, carried to Britain by Christ's uncle Joseph of Arimathea. They vowed then, one and all, to go from Camelot immediately, and never to return unless they found the Grail.

Arthur wept then, because he knew that the Fellowship was broken, and the Round Table would never have its full compliment of knights again. But he gave the companions his blessing, and that night they spent in vigil at a sacred spot close to Tintagel, where a holy man had made his home in a

Below *St Nechtan's Glen, near Tintagel. The Grail Knights began their Quest here.*

rocky valley. A great waterfall fell into a deep basin, and here they spent the night in prayer. With the dawn, they left and parted to travel to the four corners of the earth, seeking the Holy Grail of Christ's Passion.

TRADITION TELLS US that they spent their vigil at **St Nechtan's Glen** (200: SX 082882), a beautiful, peaceful spot 2m/3km north of Tintagel. The Glen ends at a set of very steep steps, and at the top is a building which stands on the site of St Nechtan's hermitage. It is said that he settled here in around 500AD, which makes him contemporary with those who fought at Badon, and that he had a silver bell set in the tower of his chapel. When the Celtic church argued with Roman doctrine, he cast the bell into the basin of the waterfall, vowing that it would not ring for unbelievers. Needless to say, it can still sometimes be heard, but its ringing is not a good omen. From the house you can approach the **Kieve** (or basin), into which the waterfall plunges some 60ft/18m before tumbling out into the stream which runs through the Glen. It is very easy to imagine, standing in a steep-sided gorge with the waterfall roaring before you, that here the knights of the Round Table contemplated both their Quest and their mortality before setting out on their journey.

St Nechtan's Kieve (basin) near Tintagel, where the Grail Knights held a vigil before setting out on their great Quest.

GLASTONBURY : THE ABBEY: ST JOSEPH'S WELL AND CRYPT

Was the Grail real, or did it exist only as a dream to be achieved in the minds of men? Oh, many are the quarrels that question has caused. For a thousand and more years the argument has raged, and still there is no end in sight. There is a tale, an old, old tale, that tells us that the Grail was real. But first, to make sense of it, we must go back further even than the first bearer of the Cup, to the days when Jesus was a child.

Before Christ became a man, in those lost years of which the Gospels do not speak, a story tells that he journeyed for a while with his uncle Joseph of Arimathea, who was a merchant. One journey brought them to the island of Britain and the land of Dumnonia, where Joseph had interests in the tin mines there. Called by an inner voice, the boy Jesus led his uncle inland by waterways and mere, until at last they reached an island of three hills, in the far eastern part of Dumnonia, now called Somerset. There Jesus said a church should be built of hurdles and daub, and when it was built, He dedicated it to his Holy Mother, Mary the Virgin. And so the first church in the world was built in Glastonbury.

THE OLD CHURCH, as it came to be called, was destroyed with the rest of the Abbey in a disastrous fire in 1184. By that time, it was built around in stone and lead, and its true origins had been completely lost. The tale of Jesus and Joseph is later than the fire, but there is no doubt that the wattle church was very ancient even when the Saxons first arrived at the abbey at Glastonbury in 658AD.

A tall wooden cross now marks the point of the Church's north-west corner. The Lady Chapel, the first part of the Abbey to be rebuilt after the fire, occupies most of its site. The crypt of this chapel was dedicated to St Joseph before the Dissolution of the Monasteries in 1539, and has been re-consecrated this century for worship. Leading off the crypt is a small passage, with a covered well at the end. This is known as St Joseph's Well, and at the time of the wattle church would have been outside. The arch now over this well is thought to be Norman but has been moved from its original location. There is no doubt that the knights of the Grail Quest would have come to Glastonbury Abbey, and perhaps taken advantage of its hospitality. Who is to say that they did not receive guidance and vision when praying in the 'Vetusta Ecclesia' (Ancient Church) of the original Grail-Bearer?

In the crypt below St Mary's Chapel, Glastonbury Abbey, is a well dedicated to Joseph of Arimathea.

THE HOLY THORN

After the Crucifixion, Joseph of Arimathea left Palestine with a small group of companions and sailed westward. They carried with them the cup which had been used by the Apostles at the Last Supper, containing some of Christ's blood which Joseph had collected from Christ as he hung upon the cross. Eventually they landed in Cornwall, where Joseph was well-known as a trader in tin, but the lords there were hostile to the new faith and so the companions travelled on. Eventually they came to the Somerset marshes and the isle where Joseph had travelled many years before with his nephew. Weary from the long journey, they stopped on the first of the hills of the island, and began to complain of their tiredness. To hearten them, Joseph thrust his hawthorn staff into the ground, where it blossomed into a glorious tree. Joyful now, they continued into the Vale of Avalon. The church Joseph had built there thirty and more years before, dedicated by Christ himself to his lady mother, was still there. But he felt that this church was wrong for the Grail, and urged them on just a little further.

WIRRAL OR **WEARYALL HILL** (182: ST 492382) is a long, low hill which snakes westwards out of Glastonbury. About half way up the townward slope stands a lone, wind-blasted thorn tree. This is said to be a descendant of the original which flowered from Joseph's staff. That tree was hacked down by a furious Puritan in the seventeenth century, and a stone now marks the spot where it stood. Other descendants of the miraculous thorn – which does blossom in the depths of winter – stand outside St John's Church in Glastonbury High Street and in the grounds of Glastonbury Abbey. Sprigs of blossom are sent to the Queen every Christmas. It is interesting that offshoots of the thorn will only produce Christmas flowers if they have been propagated from cuttings. If they are taken from seeds, they revert to the normal blossoming pattern of native hawthorn. The closest relative to the Glastonbury Thorn is found in Syria . . .

The Holy Thorn, standing lonely on Wearyall Hill, Glastonbury.

WELLHOUSE LANE

When Joseph and his companions came into the shadow of the hills of Glastonbury, they found a spring which never stopped flowing, bubbling up from the foot of the great Tor. Here, in the valley between the two hills, they decided to build a chapel to house the Holy Grail which they had carried with them from Palestine. This church was built with wattle and daub, and when the daub was dry the walls were painted white, so that the Grail Chapel glowed against the green of the hill. And they built cells for themselves, and guarded the Grail in Glastonbury.

THERE IS SOME ARGUMENT as to whether the author of the 'High History of the Holy Grail' was referring to the Old Church (which became the nucleus for the later Abbey) when describing the location for the Grail Chapel. The author has decided to make them separate places, as the Old Church was said to have been built some 30

Above The White Spring in Glastonbury. A cafe now protects the ancient water supply.

years before the Arimathean's arrival with the Grail.

In **Wellhouse Lane**, which is the modern, tarmacked equivalent of the valley between the hills', remains were found of a small monastic community probably housing only three monks, living as hermits in the old Celtic style. Whether they were separate from the known community on the top of the Tor, as well as from the Abbey, we have no way of guessing. Certainly, they protected the water supply for both communities. They might well have had their own chapel, laying the basis for the whitewashed Grail Chapel of the legend. The spring itself is now part of the Chalice Well Gardens.

After many years, the Grail Cup disappeared. Some said it had passed from this world completely; others claimed that it had been given to other, mortal Guardians. Yet others said that Joseph, or his descendants, buried the Grail on Chalice Hill near the spring, and that is why the waters run red. For this reason, the spring at the foot of the hill is called the Red or Blood Spring.

Right *Chalice Well Gardens, Glastonbury. The waterfall in 'King Arthur's Courtyard' runs red with the blood of the Holy Grail.*

JUST BEFORE the turn into Wellhouse Lane from Chilkwell Street is the entrance to the **Chalice Well Gardens.** Here, a series of beautifully landscaped gardens climbs to the well-head, which has a cover decorated with the 'Vesica Piscis'. This device, of two interlocking circles, was designed by Frederick Bligh Bond, an archaeologist and psychic questor of the early twentieth century. The lid covers the ancient well-house which houses the waters of the Red Spring and was once above ground. Stonework within the well-house is, on the whole, medieval. Silting of the valley in the last few centuries has

Below *Chalice Well Gardens, Glastonbury. The well head is covered by this lid. The design is known as the 'vesica piscis'.*

Chalice Well Gardens, Glastonbury. The Lion's Head is the only place where the water is drinkable. It is set in a sanctuary area, where modern day pilgrims might sit in private meditation.

raised the soil level by several feet, completely burying the medieval building.

From the well-head, one passes through a peaceful expanse of lawn to the Sanctuary, where the waters of the Spring flow from a lion's head. This is the only point in the enclosure where the water is safe to drink, and is designated as a 'quiet' area for private contemplation.

Below this again is 'King Arthur's Courtyard' with a beautiful waterfall and the Pilgrim's Bath, where the sick came in previous centuries to bathe in the curative waters of the Red Spring. Above the gate one again finds the device of the Vesica Piscis in wrought iron, pierced by a sword meant to be Excalibur.

Beside a giant yew tree, thought to be the descendant of an avenue of paired yews which have grown here since at least Roman times, the spring tumbles through a series of small basins into two shallow, interlocking pools, forming the Vesica Piscis once more. Everywhere the spring flows is stained a deep red, emphasising the legend of blood in the well.

ST MICHAEL'S MOUNT AND MARAZION

Before Arthur was born, two giants lived on Carrick Luz en Cuz. The husband, Cormoran, decided to build a church there, and insisted that it must be made of white stone. The stone had to be carried for a great distance, and his wife grew tired. One night while her husband slept, she brought a piece of greenstone from a much closer quarry. But Cormoran would have none of it, and threw the rock at her. Though it missed, it landed beside the road, and can still be seen there today. They say Arthur slew Cormoran, but that was another giant and another Mount of Michael, over the sea.

ST MICHAEL'S MOUNT (203: SW 515298) rises from Mount's Bay in the south of Cornwall like a miniature replica of Mont Saint-Michel in France. It is part of the 'lost land' of Lyonesse, Tristan's birthplace, now drowned under the Atlantic Ocean. Its old Cornish name means 'the ancient rock in the wood', a reference to the fact that Mount's Bay was once a forest. Extremely low tides have, indeed, revealed remains of a petrified forest between the Mount and the shore. It has been suggested that St Michael's Mount was the location of the Grail Castle. While this is difficult to prove, the link between the Grail and the Virgin Mary which threads through all the Grail

St Michael's Mount, Cornwall. Many legends of Arthur have been transferred here from Mont Saint-Michel in France. It could be the site of the Grail Castle.

Legends is here in Cornwall: the greenstone rock dropped by Cormoran's wife is known as Chapel Rock, and there was once a shrine there to Mary. Tenuous, yes, but no more so than any of the Grail Quest locations.

The causeway to the Mount runs from **Marazion** (203: SW 515306). A legend of the Trevilian family tells how, in the Middle Ages, the head of the family was riding through the forest when he heard a great rushing of waves. He escaped the inundation of the land by riding wildly ahead of the waves, scrambling ashore at Marazion. The family coat-of-arms shows a horse rearing from the water. Finds from the area now underwater between the Isles of Scilly, off the Cornish coast, have shown evidence of occupation at least up to the fourth century AD, which means this area must still have been dry land in Roman times.

St Michael's Mount and Causeway, Cornwall. Mount's Bay was once a forest in the land of Lyonesse, where Tristan was born.

CHAPTER SIX

And Britain Cried Out, "He is Gone!"

Arthur's Death and Grave

From the land of mists and waters came she
To the land of mortals and men
Her dowry it was the dawn of new hope
Her conquest, the greatest of men
Her gift was a sword, that greatest of swords
Whose wielder would ne'er come to grief
And the man to whose care she entrusted this sword
Was Arthur, my Lord and my Liege

Out of the darkening forest rode she
Over the waters so still
Down into the depths of her watery realm
To wait for the moment death's knell
Brought back to her that greatest of men
While Britain cried out, "He is gone!"
We know he but sleeps the sleep that heals all
In the darkened halls of Avalon

(Val Joice)

What to tell of the final battle, that they call the strife of Camlann? A sorry tale however you term it, for it wasn't a great battle like Badon, just a useless, pitiful excuse for a battle, and it wiped out the flower of the British and left the way open for the Saxons to conquer us, and worst of all, it took Artos from us forever. And all because Mordred, may his name be damned, wanted the throne and the queen for himself. After the Grail Quest was over, so very few of the knights returned, and the Round Table was broken. Those few of Arthur's men who survived grew old, as did the king himself. There were younger men at court now, and they were restless, and wanted adventure, but they would not quest for it the way the old men had. It was Mordred who led them in their muttering, Mordred the king's nephew, who had insulted the queen by striking her at Kelliwic and had his fortress destroyed for his pains. And when Arthur sailed to Britanny, Mordred took his chance, spreading rumours that the king was dead and seizing the throne – and Gwenhwyfar – for himself.

Arthur returned and called the faithful to him, and marched to Camelot to regain what was his. Some say that there was to be a treaty, or that Mordred was to be exiled, and that the battle only started because some young idiot drew his sword to kill a snake. I don't care. I don't care how it started! It started, on

Camlann's lonely strand, in the mist of an October dawn, and it need never have been! All day they fought, Briton against Briton, and finally the two generals met. Arthur dealt Mordred a mighty blow, and that should have been the end, but the enemy had strength to deal one final stroke, and Arthur fell. Do you hear me?

Arthur fell.

Few came away from Camlann strand. Bedwyr the faithful, Arthur's brother in arms since those long ago days with Cadwy at Dindraethou, was entrusted with one last charge: to cast Excalibur into the mere that lay close by. Twice he tried, and returned to the Pendragon's side, and both times Arthur asked what he had seen. Both times he replied, "Nothing, my Lord." And Arthur sent him again.

The third time, Bedwyr hurled the sword far out into the water, and a woman's hand clothed in white samite rose from the waves and caught it, brandishing it three times in the air before sinking below the surface once more.

With Excalibur gone, Arthur seemed content to wait for the barge that came gliding over the water, with three weeping queens at its helm. They took him into the barge and sailed west, into the evening mist, towards Avalon.

Oh Artos, Artorius, Arthur. You are gone, and Britain weeps for you still.

SLAUGHTERBRIDGE

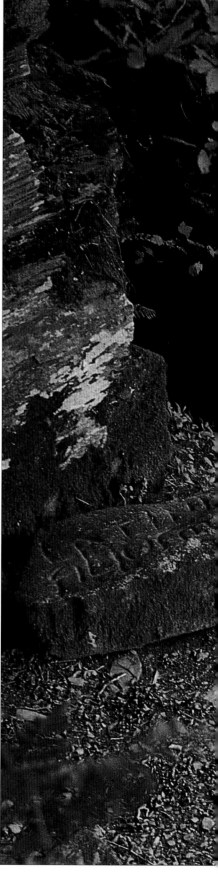

CAMLANN may have been fought in Cornwall or in Somerset. All evidence, including the original Latin reference, implies that it was a skirmish rather than a full-scale battle, and tradition makes it a civil strife between Arthur and 'Medraut'. Only the legend makes them enemies or relatives: they might even have been on the same side.

If 'Camlann strand' was in Cornwall, only one area seems to hold a really strong claim to be the battle-site. This is **Slaughterbridge** (200: SX 110855), near Camelford. The claim and tradition can be traced back to Geoffrey of Monmouth, who places the battle at the 'River Camblam' (Camel). The battle was said to have taken place in the water meadow by the river. Arthur, mortally wounded by Mordred's poisoned sword, stumbled upstream and finally perished where now lies an inscribed stone.

The inscription reads: 'LATINI ICIACIT FILIUS M . . . AR . . .', with the last, weathered letters being variously interpreted by different scholars. The most accepted reading is 'MAGARI', which would make the inscription translate as 'Latinus lies here, the son of Magarus'. In the sixteenth century, however, the name was locally considered to be 'ATRY', which they took as a debased version of Arthur. There was a mighty battle fought in this area, but it was one of the last stands of the native Cornish against the invading Saxons, in 823AD – 300 years too late for Arthur.

Below and right The inscribed stone near Slaughterbridge in Cornwall, said to commemmorate Arthur. Arthur's final battle may have been fought nearby.

DOZMARY POOL AND LOE POOL

AFTER CAMLANN, the tale tells us that Arthur begged Bedwyr to throw Excalibur back into the lake nearby. Cornwall has two main contenders for this lake. The nearest is some 7 miles/11km from Slaughterbridge, which seems a very long way for an injured man to travel, even to do his lord's bidding. For him to do so three times, as the legend tells us, is almost beyond belief . . . **Dozmary Pool** (201: SX 195745) is a lake in the middle of Bodmin Moor, near to Bolventor and Daphne Du Maurier's Jamaica Inn. It was said to be bottomless, adding to its mystique and explaining why Excalibur had never been found. In fact, it dried up completely in 1859. Presumably, few people have mentioned its fathomless quality since then.

If it seems unlikely that Bedwyr would crawl or stumble 7 miles to throw away a sword, however magical, then the other candidate for the mere is even more incredible. **Loe Pool** (203: SW 643242) is an inlet – actually an 'inland lake' separated from the sea by a narrow strip of land – on Mount's Bay, near Helston and 40 miles/64.4km from the only Cornish possibility for Camlann. Even on a horse, it is unlikely that Bedwyr could have made his fabled journey before Arthur expired. It was, however, the probable inspiration behind Tennyson's description of the home of the Lady of the Lake.

Below Dozmary Pool. a haunted place on Bodmin Moor, is said to be bottomless.

Right Sea view across Mount's Bay from Loe Bar. Bedwyr may have cast Excalibur into the mere from this spot.

Giant's Grave, Arthur's Bed and Trethevy Quoit

THE **GIANT'S GRAVE** (190: SX 202908) is a long, low mound, possibly neolithic, within the ramparts of Warbstow Bury hillfort, just north of the A395. It has more recently been alternatively named Arthur's Grave. Neither the double ramparted fort nor the mound have any Arthurian archaeology associated with them, and it is thought that the link with Arthur came about because of the proximity (8 miles/13km) to Camelford and Slaughterbridge.

Arthur's Bed (201: SX 240757) is a flat stone on Bodmin Moor, formed from the local granite. One of many such in the area, it can be difficult to locate without photographs. Centuries of wind and rain have weathered the surface into the likeness of an open-topped stone coffin, and the stone, like many other natural features, has been adopted by local folk as having an Arthurian connection.

Trethevy Quoit (201: SX 259689) is also known as Arthur's Quoit, but is actually the remains of a neolithic burial chamber about 300 years old. It can be found between St Cleer and Darite, off the B3254 near Liskeard. It has partially collapsed now, but remains impressive. It was probably once covered by an earth mound. The only Arthurian connection is the name.

Neither of these sites can realistically be considered Arthur's final resting place – if, indeed, he did die, and is not sleeping in a cave under a hill, as many believe. It is Somerset which has the best claim to Arthur's grave.

Left Arthur's Bed, Bodmin Moor. This granite outcrop has been weathered into a coffin shape.

Below Arthur's Grave, Warbstowbury, Cornwall. This is probably a neolithic burial mound.

*Trethevy Quoit, near Liskeard,
Cornwall. This impressive monument is
neolithic and would once have been
covered by an earthen mound. One of
the upright stones is pierced, allowing
access to the centre. It is also known as
Arthur's Quoit, despite having no
historical connection to the King.*

RIVER CAM

THE **RIVER CAM** (183: ST 620259) flows through the village of Little Weston just south of Sparkford and the A303 through Somerset. It is within walking distance of the still mighty and impressive Cadbury Castle, possible home of Arthur and his 'brave heroes'. Although almost sleepy now, the river Cam is a likely site for the 'strife of Camlann'. In the nineteenth century, a farmer reported finding, in a meadow called Westwoods, the bones of many men still with their weapons and armour, crouched in the western shadow of the hill. Although this report has never, unfortunately, been substantiated, it adds credence to the legends that Arthur fought his last battle close to his home.

The picturesque River Cam flows through the Somerset countryside near South Cadbury. The bones of warriors found nearby in the last century gave substance to the legend that the battle of Camlann was fought here.

SOMERSET LEVELS, RIVER BRUE, POMPARLES BRIDGE AND WEARYALL HILL

Let us follow Arthur, my friends, on his final journey. From Cadbury and the River Cam, after the battle was over and his people realised that he was mortally wounded, he was laid gently on a barge which sailed north-eastwards towards the great cone of Glastonbury Tor. In order that the people could witness his journey, the barge landed near the church of Lantokai in the place which is now called Street, and the sad procession continued along the old Roman road across the causeway to the Pons Perilis, which crosses the River Brue near Beckery. Here, at Arthur's bidding, Bedwyr carried out an ancient Celtic ceremony. The sword which his lord had carried into battle for most of his adult life was 'killed', bent beyond repair, and cast into the mere which surrounded the Holy Isle of Avalon.

The procession of the wounded Pendragon continued, up on to Wearyall Hill, past the Holy Thorn planted, some say, by Joseph of Arimathea himself, and at last rested for a while at the convent of St Peter, where Arthur had dreamt of the Virgin many years before.

Later, with his wife and his sisters grieving a death that none had yet witnessed, he was taken in secret to the abbey and the care of the monks, where the oldest church in the land was close by for prayer and vigil. No-one knows for certain whether he died, for the land was in turmoil, the Saxons marching once more, and the British would not admit – even to themselves – that their greatest hero might be mortal. One thing is certain. Arthur was never – in this life – seen again.

Left *From Wearyall Hill in Glastonbury, the route of Arthur's last journey from Lantokai (Street) can be traced.*

Below *Pomparles Bridge, between Glastonbury and Street, the Pons Perilis of legend from which Bedwyr cast Excalibur into the River Brue.*

The procession would have paused here on the summit of Wearyall Hill, where stood the convent of St Peter. Below the hill is the modern town of Glastonbury, where the grievously wounded king was entrusted to the care of the monks of the Abbey.

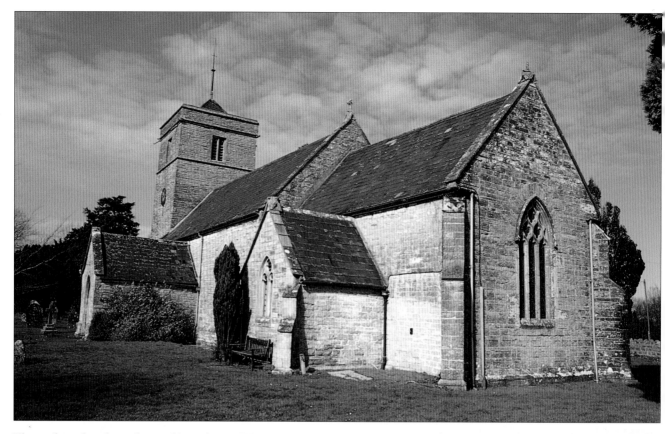

The modern church on the outskirts of Street, near Glastonbury, probably stands on the site of a sixth century hermitage. Arthur's barge would have made landfall here, at Lantokai.

Even today, we can follow this last, sad journey. The aspects have changed beyond recognition, for the Vale of Avalon is now dry meadowland where once it was mere and lake, but the atmosphere can still be felt.

'**Lantokai**' (182: ST 488372) is the old name for Leigh, in Street, and was the site of a hermit's chapel in the fifth century. This was probably on the site of the modern church on the Glastonbury side of Street, and would have been at the head of the old Roman causeway some metres to the east of the modern A39.

The Pons Perilis is now marked as **Pomparles Bridge** (182: ST 487378), an unremarkable structure which replaced a more impressive medieval bridge. When the Brue floods, however, the imagination can see Bedwyr hurling the sword away.

From Pomparles, one can enter Glastonbury via Beckery, past the new sewage works; straight along the A39; along the 'Roman Way' which was probably the oldest route into the town; or over **Wearyall Hill** on foot. From the top of Wearyall, one can look back over the Somerset Levels towards Lantokai and Cadbury, and forward to the Abbey and, supposedly, Arthur's last resting place. Pass the Holy Thorn, where perhaps the procession paused in prayer, and come out over a stile opposite modern houses which now form Hill Head. It was here that the 'convent of St Peter' was said to be.

Glastonbury Abbey: the Old Cemetery and Arthur's Tomb

1191 AD: a Welsh bard let it be known to the king of England that Arthur, once King of the Britons, was buried in the cemetery of Glastonbury Abbey, deep under the earth between two pyramids. The Abbey was being raised again to the Glory of God at that time, after the conflagration which had razed it to the ground. On the order of the king, the monks there dug between the two pyramids, and seven feet below the surface they found a leaden cross, inscribed:

HIC IACIT SEPULTUS INCLITUS REX ARTURIUS IN INSULA AVALONIA

Ever further they dug, and at last found an ancient wooden coffin made from a hollowed tree-trunk. Lifting this to the surface, they opened the lid, and found the bones of a very tall man, well over six feet in height, and at his feet the bones of a small woman and a lock of golden hair, which crumbled at the touch of a curious brother. And they knew that the bard and the cross together had spoken true:

HERE LIES THE BODY OF THE RENOWNED KING ARTHUR IN THE ISLAND OF AVALON

1278 AD: King Edward and his Queen visited the mighty Abbey of Glaston, and viewed the bones of King Arthur and his Lady, Guinevere. These relics were moved from their place of honour where they had been kept for almost a century since their discovery, and placed in a magnificent black marble tomb before the High Altar, where all might now marvel at and venerate them.

IN 1962, excavations led by Dr Ralegh Radford in the grounds of the abbey found the unmistakeable traces of that long ago search, and the base of the tomb in which the coffin was found. These traces were at approximately the correct depth (7ft/2.13km) from the medieval ground level. Analysis of the soil proved that the exhumation could only have taken place during the time of the

Glastonbury Abbey glows red-gold in the sunset. The Abbey was said to be Arthur's burial place.

Abbey rebuilding, around 1190 or 1191. The 'leaden cross', now lost, would have lain at the ground level of the tenth century, which was then artificially raised during the abbacy of St Dunstan (940-957). This would account for the seven feet of earth before the cross was found. There is no trace now of the 'two pyramids', but the ancient cemetery lay directly south of the **Lady Chapel** as it now stands, alongside the cloisters. The site of the original tomb is no longer marked.

The plaque which we now see marking **Arthur's Grave** is on the site of the base of the marble tomb of 1278. This was destroyed at the Dissolution, and the bones were irretrievably lost.

After Arthur left the world, whether he died and was buried as they tell us, or whether he still lies sleeping in a cave, those who survived him had to choose what they would do with their lives. Gwenhwyfar, who had been ruled by her passions and excited desire in so many others, retired to the nunnery at Amesbury, and so brought the story full circle. That place where Ambrosius and Uther had been buried by the Giant's Dance on Salisbury Plain, so many weary years before, now became home to Arthur's widow.

Lancelot and Bedwyr came separately to the chapel and house of a hermit, and dwelt there for the rest of their lives in seclusion and prayer. Some believe that this chapel was that which had housed the Grail when it was solid, and real, at the foot of Glastonbury Tor. I would like to think so, for then they would have remained close to the living memory of the Pendragon.

Left *South wall of Lady Chapel, Glastonbury Abbey. The Old Cemetery lay alongside this wall, in the middle ground of the picture. Arthur would have been buried here.*

Right *This unremarkable plot of land in Glastonbury Abbey marks the site of an exquisite marble tomb, built in 1278 to house the royal remains.*

Overleaf *Glastonbury Abbey ruins, looking west down the length of the Abbey church. The fenced-off rectangular area is the site of the High Altar, with Arthur's tomb beyond.*

The British lands and the mantle of High King came to Constantine, who was young and untried. He worked and fought hard, but God knows he was no Arthur. It was but a few years before the Saxons whom we had struggled to keep back for so long pushed forward again, and they won Dumnonia in the end. They call us foreigners, and slaves, for that is what 'Welsh' means in their barbarian tongue. We don't forget. We keep the flame high. One day, we say. One day.

In the night, men are waiting
In the mountains of the dawn
For the call, they are waiting
For the sound of Dragon's horn
In the dreams of western shadows
Shines the light of hopeful flame
In the east, the darkness gathers
Poised to drown the Light's domain

In the hall, we see the shadows
In our hearts, the flame burns strong
For the west, Red Dragon Banner
For the Light, keep burning long
Many dreams have been shattered
Yet here we stand, proud and free
Where the hope grows ever stronger
And we dream of victory

And the Light will drown the shadows
And the west will claim its own
Keep the flame forever burning
For this land, our island home
And remember candle burning
And the Light which once flared high
Shed no tears, have patience waiting
For the flame can never die.

Denise Stobie and Val Joice

The Glass Isle sleeps in the light of a full moon. Glastonbury Tor still evokes the magic and mystery of ancient Avalon.

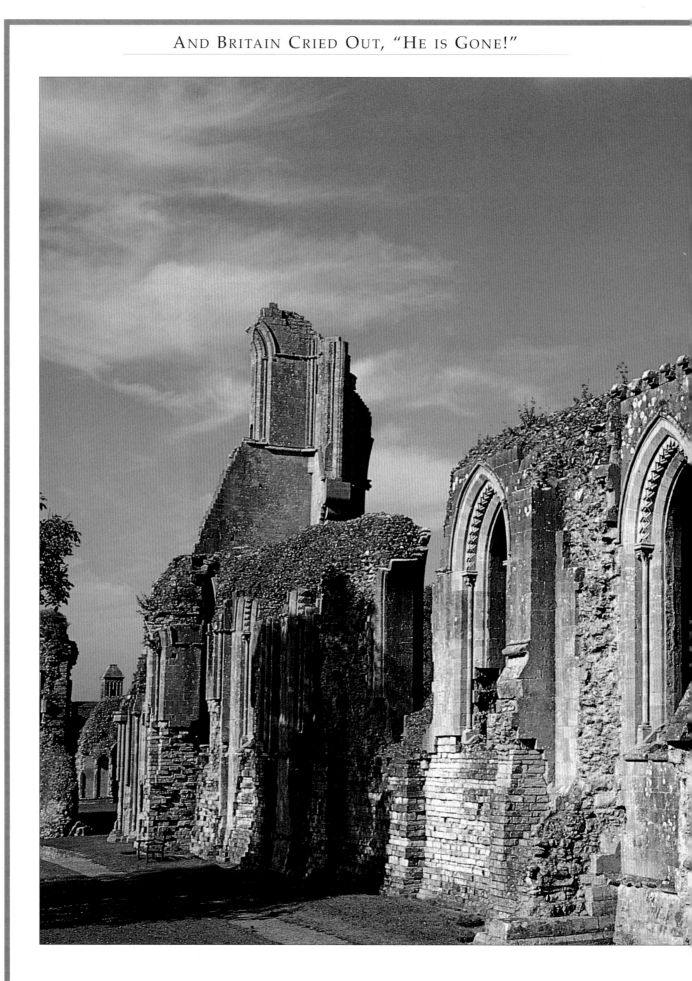

Glastonbury Abbey. These medieval remains cover the site of the earliest church in Britain, which inspired Blake's hymn 'Jerusalem'. Beside this ancient chapel, Arthur and Guinevere were buried in a coffin made from a hollowed out oak tree.

SELECTED BIBLIOGRAPHY

ALCOCK, L, *'By South Cadbury is that Camelot. . .'* Book Club Associates. 1973

ASHE, G, *Avalonian Quest.* Book Club Associates. 1982

ASHE, G, *From Caesar To Arthur.* Collins. 1960

ASHE, G, *King Arthur In Fact and Legend.* Thomas Nelson Inc. 1971

ASHE, G, *King Arthur's Avalon.* Book Club Associates. 1974

ASHE, G, *The Quest For Arthur's Britain.* Pall Mall Press. 1969

ASHE, G, *The Traveller's Guide to Arthurian Britain.* Gothic Image Publications. 1997

ASHTON, G, *The Realm of King Arthur.* J Arthur Dixon. 1974

CHAMBERS, E K, *Arthur of Britain.* Sidgwick & Jackson. 1966

COGHLAN, R, *Encyclopædia of Arthurian Legends.* Element Books. 1991

ELLIOTT-CANNON, A, *In Quest of King Arthur.* Quest Publications. 1976

EVANS, S (trans), *The High History of the Holy Grail.* James Clarke & Co Ltd. 1969

FRASER, A, *King Arthur.* Sidgwick & Jackson. 1970

GEOFFREY OF MONMOUTH, *History of the Kings of Britain.* Penguin. 1973

HOGG, A H A, *A Guide to the Hillforts of Britain.* Paladin. 1975

LACY, N J & ASHE, G, *The Arthurian Handbook.* Garland Publishing, Inc. 1988

LACY, N J (ed), *The New Arthurian Encyclopædia.* Garland Publishing, Inc. 1991

MALORY, T, *Le Morte D'Arthur Vols I &II.* Penguin. 1977

MATTHEWS, C, *Arthur and the Sovereignty of Britain.* Arkana. 1989

MATTHEWS, C & J, *The Arthurian Book of Days.* Sidgwick & Jackson. 1990

MATTHEWS, J, *King Arthur's Britain: A Photographic Odyssey.* Blandford Press. 1995

MATTHEWS, J, *The Grail Tradition.* Element Books. 1990

MATTHEWS, J & STEWART, RJ, *Warriors of Arthur.* Blandford Press. 1987

MEYRICK, J, *Holy Wells of Cornwall.* J Meyrick. 1982

MORRIS, J, *The Age of Arthur.* Weidenfeld & Nicholson. 1989

RAHTZ, P, *English Heritage Book of Glastonbury.* Batsford. 1993

STEWART, M, *The Crystal Cave.* Hodder & Stoughton. 1970

STEWART, M, *The Hollow Hills.* Hodder & Stoughton. 1973 ·

STEWART, M, *The Last Enchantment.* Hodder & Stoughton. 1979

STEWART, R J & MATTHEWS, J, *Legendary Britain.* Blandford Press. 1989

TENNYSON, A Lord, *The Idylls of the King.* Collins. 1956

WOOLF, C, *Introduction to the Archaeology of Cornwall.* D Bradford Barton Ltd. 1970